# Once Broken


by

(Author)

Disclaimer



The purpose of this eBook is to educate. The author and the publisher do not warrant that the information contained in this e-book is fully complete and shall not be responsible for any errors or omissions. The author and publisher shall have neither liability nor responsibility to any person or entity concerning any loss or damage caused or alleged to be caused directly or indirectly by this e-book.

# Table of Contents

# Introduction

There comes a time in everyone's life when they face something that completely breaks them, like trusting people we shouldn't have. Investing our love and care in a relationship that is not worth it. It can even be a failure. We try our best only to lose in the end. We fail and fail yet again despite giving everything in our power.

These events become life-changing for us.

You must have faced something like that, too.

Something that makes you think you are beyond repair. Darkness surrounds you, and it seems like there is no light at the end of the tunnel. This darkness consumes you, convincing you that nothing can ever be good again.

At this point, you have two choices:

1. Continue living in this void until all will and hope are lost, and you are simply a part of nothingness.

OR

2. Heal and restore your mind, body, and soul to rejuvenate and become whole again.

While the latter may seem impossible, this impossibility cannot be further from the truth. We don't give the human spirit enough credit. Humans have resilience ingrained in them. All you need to do is channel it.

Even a quarter of that determination can be enough to start working on personal transformation. According to Maslow's Theory of Motivation, humans are at peak level when they reach self-actualization.

He believed that once people fulfill their bodily and ego needs, they reach self-actualization, where they are at peace with themselves.

But that is not all you need to reach the peak. Not to mention, getting to this point is the main struggle, isn't it?

This path is often laden with pain, suffering, and much reflection. It is only then that you find your Eden. Contrary to popular belief, this Eden isn't reserved for only special people.

*We all have the potential to heal and grow from our pain.*

*We all have the power to learn from our lives and go through personal transformation by giving our all.*

*We all have the strength to draw a specific element from our pain that helps us restore and visualize ourselves in a better position in life.*

Just like you, I, too, at one point, was standing at this crossroad, staring at the path I could take.

Betrayed.

Lost.

Unloved.

I had lost the will to live; I was merely surviving each day, trying to make it through until bedtime, only to wake up feeling miserable yet again.

People I once held close and trusted had turned away from me. I was alone with no one to go to but myself.

This made me see that I was the only one who could help me. No one was coming to the rescue.

I found a peculiar power within me, gasping for breath and urging me to hold on. I found the will I needed to rise another day with the passion and energy I once had.

This resilience and this strength pushed me to learn about myself and go on a path of miraculous discovery that led me to my transformation.

This book entails my journey to gaining that strength, power, and will to carry you forward from your suffering. Through this story, I hope to show you that if others can find this strength, so can you. I hope to inspire you to look within and consider this book a guide to learning to piece yourself together, restore, and heal by finding the inner strength that will help you grow into having a strong mind, body, and soul.

As you progress from the beginning to the end of our story, this book will help you escape the darkness and leap toward the light.

Are you ready to begin your path to resilience and personal transformation?

# Chapter 1: Fragments of Pain

Sara Marvin is a shy girl who has trouble making connections with people because of being socially awkward and an introvert. At 27, most people found it unbelievable that she hadn't dated or been in a relationship since she graduated college.

She felt it was mentally exhausting for her to form meaningful relationships only to be left with pain in the end.

Sara was 17 when her best friend spilled the gossip that her crush, Richi Lionel, wanted to take Sara to the prom. It was their last year at high school, and Sara had managed to spend her school life without going through a heartbreak. Megan, Sara's best friend, reminded her that she was young and beautiful and deserved to get some attention on this special day.

So, when Richi approached to ask her to the prom, she said yes. Sara's mom and Megan fussed over her a lot; taking her shopping to buy a beautiful dress and a new pair of shoes, Sara felt overwhelmed.

Unfortunately, that was the only fun part of this experience. All night at the prom, Richi spent his time convincing his ex-girlfriend to get back together with him.

Sara felt humiliated and decided to leave early. She cried her eyes out at home and decided to avoid dating and relationships altogether. She didn't want to feel this pain again.

She stayed true to her vow for several years, and then, as luck would have it, Sara befriended a guy from her class in college. Greg McKowley was like Sara, an introvert. He was by himself mostly, and the only reason the two spoke to each other was a group project. Friendship bloomed into a very serious relationship, and they decided to rent an apartment and move in together after graduation.

Being a handsome guy, he attracted much attention from other girls, but that never bothered her. Greg's attention was always on Sara; he showered her with care and affection (and presents) occasionally. She found herself opening up to him and bared her soul. Sara had her lady friends, but being with someone in an intimate relationship was different. She felt like she had found her soul mate. Greg was someone who understood her and respected her feelings.

Greg often went out with his friends, leaving Sara behind since he knew she wasn't comfortable being around people. Sara trusted Greg with all her heart.

Soon, they found a nice and cozy apartment to move into. This was the start of a new phase in their life. The future looked bright, and Sara felt Greg was *the one*. She never thought she could find someone like him.

One night, a friend messaged her a picture as she sat in bed, reading her novel. As she clicked on the image, the world around her stood still.

It was a shot of Greg sitting intimately with a girl in a bar. She couldn't believe it. It has to be photoshopped! That couldn't be Greg. He was out with his friends.

Sara immediately Facetimed her friend. A video call couldn't lie. Could it?

Sara's friend sneakily showed her Greg sitting with the girl. She didn't need to see more. She hung up the call and instantly got in a car.

Tears streamed down Sara's face as she drove the car. She hurried inside, trembling. Her friend led her to Greg's table, who was nuzzling the strange woman's neck. She was giggling.

Sara just stared at him.

"Sara! What are you… Listen, I can explain," he blabbered.

She couldn't hear a word. The bar spun around. She could hear her friend saying something to Greg. She looked into his eyes, unable to utter a word. She took off the promise ring he had jokingly given her at a carnival once and threw it in his face.

Back at home, she bawled her eyes out. All those times he said he was going out, is this what he was doing? Was he out with this girl every time? Or was it different girls?

How long had this been going on? How long had he been cheating on her?

Was it her?

Was she not enough for him? Did he not love her anymore?

Was Sara not beautiful enough? Was he not attracted to her anymore?

A hundred thoughts were running in her mind. Her trust in him had shattered in seconds. She would never have believed it if she hadn't seen it with her own eyes.

She had thought they had something special. She thought she would spend all her life with him.

And now here she was at 27.

Alone.

Unable to trust people.

Soul shattered.

Getting your heart broken after investing so much in a relationship can be devastating. But it's not always a romantic relationship where your heart gets broken.

Some of us get cheated by our friends, too.

Amir Johnson lived a good life. He worked as a real estate agent at a reputable company and made an excellent annual figure that helped him live his lavish lifestyle.

Amir was a very cheerful person. He would make connections in a matter of minutes, and these connections would turn into solid friendships that he so cherished.

He wore his heart on his sleeve and was always there for his friends, offering them emotional and financial support whenever needed. Amir believed that if the universe had given him something, he owed it to the world to give it back. His empathetic nature made him a good person, and he trusted people very quickly.

Amir had gone through a few adverse experiences in friendship like everyone does, but never had he experienced something that would put him off making spontaneous connections and socializing with an open heart and mind.

That was going to change.

Amir was a helpful person, as we have established. So, when a friend, Rahul, called asking him to meet urgently, Amir couldn't ignore the distress in his voice.

He immediately requested an early off and went over to see his friend. Rahul looked entirely out of sorts and kept looking over his shoulder. He explained how he had taken a hefty loan for his business and couldn't return the money.

"They are after me, man. They might even be following me," Rahul said anxiously.

"We can figure this out. I can help you with it. We will get a good lawyer. I'll set up a meeting with the bank and..." explained Amir helpfully.

"It… it isn't the bank," answered Rahul. "It was…I found a guy on the internet and they said they would give me a $75,000 loan. They are threatening me now, man."

Amir was baffled. Rahul was a competent man. He couldn't believe someone like him could make this mistake. "Alright, we need to go to the police right now!"

"No! They are threatening me, bro. Amir, please, I just need to show them some money. If I show them that I have the money, then they will give me some time to repay the full loan. They are threatening me, man. I just need to throw some money at them. I have a payment coming in next week. I'll return your money to you as soon as I get that payment." urged Rahul.

Amir couldn't see his friend in so much trouble. He recalled the time when his aunt, who was visiting the States, had gotten in an accident, and Rahul had paid at the hospital without Amir even asking for it.

Amir hadn't been in the right senses. Seeing his aunt bleeding out had sent him into shock. Rahul took over, and Amir was grateful to him for that.

Although Amir instantly paid Rahul back, he still thought he owed Rahul for the gesture.

So, he took out his checkbook and wrote Rahul a check worth a whopping $30,000. This would put a remarkable dent in his savings, leaving him with peanuts, but Amir didn't care. He had to help his friend. Rahul was clearly in trouble.

Amir handed over the check, asking Rahul to promise they would go to the police after Rahul gave them this money.

Promising him, Rahul hurried off.

The next day, Amir messaged Rahul but got no reply. Amir left him several voice messages and was starting to get worried when he didn't hear anything from Rahul, and three days had passed.

Is Rahul okay? Did something happen to him?

Did those guys hurt him?

Amir's heart beat fast, and he drove to Rahul's place. He knocked at his door, but there was no answer. Worried, he ran to Rahul's jewelry shop, which was nearby.

He was surprised to see it closed in the middle of the day. He tried to see in but could only see darkness. Amir asked the neighboring shops, and they informed him that Rahul hadn't opened the shop for the last four days.

Amir didn't know what to do. He was worried for his friend. Amir didn't care about the money. He just wanted Rahul to be safe.

He could only think of one solution: going to the police.

What else could he do? Amir didn't know Rahul's relatives, and from what Rahul had described, these people he took the loan from seemed dangerous. What if they had kidnapped Rahul or attacked him? What if something worse had happened?

No!

Amir couldn't even fathom the thought.

Telling the police was the best thing to do for his friend.

When Amir explained to the police, they suggested something he hadn't even thought about for a second.

Rahul had stolen the money.

"That's absurd! My friend is in danger. He could possibly be lying dead in a ditch right now," retorted Amir angrily. He couldn't believe how callous the police were being. Instead of springing into action as he had hoped for, the police were suggesting something appalling and taking it as a mere case of thievery.

"Sir, we understand that, and we will do everything in our power to find him. But we do have to think from every angle. We suggest you do too," said the officer, standing up; he put a hand on his shoulder as if wrapping it up. The officer didn't, however, realize the abstract weight he was putting on Amir.

Rahul had been right. It was useless going to the police. Guilt took over, and Amir couldn't help but wonder if things could have been different if he had accompanied Rahul.

Instead of returning to work, Amir returned to his home and slumped into his couch. He repeatedly tried Rahul's number, but there was still no response.

He was imagining the worst possible scenarios.

A week passed, and this mystery had taken over his mind. He was stalking Rahul's social media, trying to figure out who he had taken the loan from and where Rahul was right now.

The police were tracking Rahul's phone, but his last location was near his shop in his neighborhood, and then the trail just vanished.

Nobody had seen him or knew where he had gone. It was like he had vanished into thin air. Amir couldnt help but take some responsibility for it.

It seemed Amir was the only person he had reached out to before he disappeared. Amir thought he could have done more. This thought had him bound.

He could have done more.

Somehow.

Amir had no idea that more was coming his way. Something that would break him entirely.

Sara and Amir's pasts were morbid. At this point, they were contemplating whether they had done enough for the people they cared for.

Had Sara loved him enough?

Could Amir have done more for him?

They were both stuck in a rut

, blaming themselves.

Were they right to do so?

They both felt broken and lost. They had no idea where they would go from here. It seemed they had hit rock bottom.

It isn't a strange feeling, is it? You and I have been there when we asked ourselves: Could this get any worse?

The world around us has lost meaning, and we are wondering how we will move on from this. How much strength will we need?

We question every decision that brought us here and blame ourselves for not being more vigilant or for being so naive. Sara and Amir were going through the same feelings.

The universe looks at you, smiles, and says, brace yourself; there is more to come.

And so it was the same for our friends, Sara and Amir. They had more sufferings coming their way. There was more they had to endure until they reached their breaking point.

# Chapter 2: The Breaking Point

Sara and Amir were caught up in their distress. Their life was haywire, and nothing seemed to give them happiness.

Greg had tried talking to Sara, but she had declared that she needed time to herself. She had thought about it and wanted to forgive him, but she just couldn't stop wondering how easy it was for Greg to deceive her.

Maybe he had lied multiple times, and she had never found out. She had a peculiar gut feeling that told her she couldn't trust Greg again. From trusting him unquestioningly to being unable to believe his words, how surreal relationships can be.

Sara still blamed herself and wondered if Greg had to resort to another woman because something was wrong with her. Perhaps they can reconcile, and Sara can change for Greg.

Or maybe it will be a mistake to trust him again. He had already lied to Sara once; who is to say he wouldn't do it again? It felt like two voices in Sara's head were arguing for and against Greg.

Standing at these crossroads, one day, she was drowning her sorrow by endlessly scrolling on Instagram when she received a DM. She opened her inbox to see a message from a stranger.

She clicked on it and saw the message was from a weird username.

iam_Brutus

She was about to ignore it, but something told her she needed to open it. Reading the message, she had mixed thoughts; she felt something in the pit of her stomach.

*"Hi Sara,*

*I didn't know if I should message you or not. I am still asking myself if this is the right thing to do, but all I know is that I have to do this.*

*I have been seeing your boyfriend, Greg, for a while now. It would be a lie to say I didn't know he was already with someone, but he never explicitly told me. I had an inkling, but I continued to ignore it because I fell in love with him.*

*Greg never talked about commitment. He never gave the impression that he was seeing me exclusively. He would get calls from other girls, probably including you, when we were together. For him, it was an open relationship; for me, it meant much more.*

*I could piece everything together. But I was hopelessly in love. I wanted to give him time to see that it was truly me with whom he belonged.*

*I want to admit that while I knew he was with other women, I thought he was casually dating them. I didn't know he was in a serious relationship with you until you moved in together.*

*A friend of mine saw you both moving into a building near her place. She told me what she saw, and I confronted Greg. I said I didn't want to continue dating if he was serious about someone else. It broke my heart to know that I wasn't the one.*

*But, and I am sorry to say this, he denied moving in with you. He told me he was merely helping you move into your new apartment and helping you set it up.*

*He said things that you are probably better off not knowing. I don't know what it was, but I didn't believe him. All the love I felt for him was gone in seconds. Despite knowing about his open relationships, I felt betrayed.*

*I blame myself for being so naive, for ever trusting him, and for thinking I could win him over.*

*I admit I was jealous of you. I stalked you to see what was so wonderful about you. What did you have that I didn't have?*

*What did he see in you that he couldn't see in me?*

*Then, you posted a picture with him. I can see you have removed it now.*

*He was looking into the camera, and you were looking at him with adoration and love. I could see cardboard boxes all around you guys. You were excited about this new life you were building with him. It broke me completely.*

*But this time, the pain I felt wasn't for me. It was for you. While you were thinking about starting this adventure, he was out there denying he loved you or that you were someone special.*

*And I knew I had to say something. I am sending you a picture of us at the Abyss. It is a dance club we went to just last Saturday.*

*I am sorry for breaking this news to you like this. I hope that someday I can meet you and apologize in person.*

*I truly am sorry, Sara."*

Sara felt like she was back at that restaurant where she caught Greg. She wanted to throw her phone out the window. She didn't think things could get worse.

Greg was like her, wasn't he? He didn't like socializing. He admitted he liked hanging around in his room the first time they met. He only went out with his friends occasionally, so where were all these girls coming from? Where was he meeting them?

Unless

it was a ruse from the beginning.

But could someone be this cruel and manipulative?

And why would he agree to move in if he didn't feel anything for Sara?

Nothing made sense.

She looked at the picture and wondered if it was even real.

All those promises for the future, were they all lies? Those cuddles, those intimate moments, all the times they kissed, and he said, I love you.

No… no… there were moments when everything was just about Greg and Sara, moments when he would make her laugh, or when he would make Sara taste something he made.

Those nights, they read together in silence, snuggled into each other.

How could she believe someone because they sent a picture? It was so easy to create a picture these days. People can use Photoshop and even AI to create whatever image they want.

She had to take matters into her own hands.

That night, she dressed in her nines. She looked closely at the picture the anonymous girl had sent her and decided to go to Abyss to find out the truth.

She made up a story about losing her purse at the nightclub last week when she visited, claiming she had some important papers in it. She sweet-talked the manager, who agreed to show her the CCTV footage.

Her stomach was in knots.

Any minute now, she would see it.

Any minute now, she would see him.

Cozying up to another girl again.

Suddenly, she saw a familiar face.

She asked the manager to pause the footage so she could take a closer look. She had felt broken when she saw Greg with another girl for the first time.

However, this time, Sara felt nothing.

The girl in the picture was there, too.

Laughing and clinging on to the love of her life.

Greg, who she trusted.

Greg, who she loved.

Greg hugged the girl back and danced with her like he had known her his whole life.

"Is that yours?" asked the manager, pointing at a handbag on the screen.

"No, I don't think so…," she replied. Thanking the manager, Sara left the club. She walked out with no destination in mind. It seemed like the world was ending, and she had lost the will to save herself.

Where could she go now? Back to the apartment? Sara had asked Greg to leave when she caught him at the restaurant. She had said she needed a break.

Being at the apartment would only remind her of what could never be. When Sara had caught Greg cheating the first time, she had thought it couldn't get worse.

She laughed at herself. It could get worse, and she was living her nightmare right now.

On the other hand, Amir was battling his mind and figuring out where Rahul could be.

He couldn't concentrate on his work. He hadn't made a sale in so long. If this continued, he would run out of the little money he had.

He was thinking of hiring a PI to track where Rahul was and the people he had last interacted with. Amir looked up a private investigator online and briefed the PI about the situation. Right when he hit send, Amir got a call. It was the police, asking to see him.

Perhaps the police found something. They wouldn't have called him otherwise, would they?

Amir left in anticipation. Somewhere in his heart, he believed he might see Rahul waiting for him at the station.

Alas, Amir did see his friend, but merely in images kept in a file.

"Is this your friend, Mr. Johnson?" the police officer asked, showing multiple images of Rahul in a foreign place. The pictures appeared to be screenshots of CCTV footage.

"Erm, yes. Looks like it," answered Amir, puzzled.

"It appears that your friend is in Uganda, sir," informed Officer Laura, the detective on the case. "Your friend, Rahul, is wanted in a case of embezzlement. He has deceived a few other friends as well. We believe you were the last person he met, and afterward, he used the help of an underground network that helped Rahul get off the grid. That is why we couldn't find him initially. We are in contact with the authorities in Uganda, and they are moving in to arrest him.

If all goes well, Mr. Rahul will be here tomorrow night."

Amir was at a loss for words.

"Erm…I think there must have been a mistake. Rahul…he had money. Why would he need to embezzle? I mean…He had a thriving business…Did you look into the people I spoke about? People he took the loan from?" asked Amir, flabbergasted.

"We haven't found any evidence suggesting this, Mr. Johnson," replied Laura. She placed a hand on Amir's shoulder and advised him to get a good lawyer.

"Sometimes we trust the wrong people. You can still get justice for what you went through," she handed Amir a lawyer's card. "He works pro bono as well," she added quietly.

Amir sat there for over an hour before an officer came over to ask if he could call someone for Amir.

Any of his friends would have agreed to come pick him up in his time of need, but he wanted to be left alone. Socializing was the last thing on his mind right now.

He had thought about the worst possible things that could have gone wrong. All he thought about was Rahul's safety. Amir couldn't believe that Rahul could deceive him like this.

Back at home, he noticed a message from the PI. The last message was Rahul explaining everything. The PI had replied in one sentence.

"I hate to say this, but I think the guy stole from you,"

Was Amir the only one who couldn't see it? Had he been so blind? Amir began questioning his intelligence and his naivety.

How could he write Rahul such a big check?

A voice in his head replied:

"Because it was never about the money. All you wanted to do was help your friend."

Indeed, for Amir, it was never about the money. There was no question about it. Rahul or any other friend could have asked for a million dollars, and Amir would have happily agreed if he had the money.

He had spent the last few weeks trying to find Rahul, figuring out what had happened and who could have hurt him, only to find out that he had stolen his money and ran away.

Betrayal can be brutal to accept at times. The police and the PI instantly understood what could have happened. While you can say it could be experience talking, all Amir could think was that his "happy to help" demeanor caused him this pain.

How could he trust people now? All these friends he had made in life. How many of them were true friends? How many of them cared for him? How many endured him to use him later when the time arrived

, Just like Rahul was biding his time.

Amir's family urged him to see a friend who was a lawyer. After all, he did have strong connections. But this overwhelming episode had him questioning the intentions of all his friends.

He decided to go to the lawyer the detective had suggested. Narrating the whole story to the lawyer was humiliating. As Amir shared the entire incident, he felt dumb. How could he not see it? It was so apparent.

"It seems you have a good heart, Mr. Johnson, and someone took advantage of that. He clearly knew how you would react and manipulated you into giving him all that money," commented Mike, the lawyer.

"Aren't you going to ask me how I could make such a stupid mistake?" inquired Amir.

"I'm a lawyer, I have seen people do worse for people they care about," he answered, smiling politely.

The case was in court for months. Eventually, justice was served. Rahul went to jail, and Mike happily bid farewell to Amir, unaware that the smile on his face was not genuine.

Amir had hit rock bottom, just like Sara.

The two, in their timelines, stopped meeting their friends. They lost the will to carry on. They felt lost and numb as if they could never make a sincere connection again.

Sara and Amir were finding it hard to get by every day.

Sara had blocked Greg. She needed no explanation. There was nothing he could say that could make her feel better. He tried sending her emails and messages and called her from different numbers, trying to get a hold of her.

But Sara was adamant. She didn't want to hear from him, much less see him.

She had concealed herself from the world. She found a new apartment and moved in a matter of days. The few days she had to live there were suffocating. Sara and Greg had made plans for every corner and every room.

Her last night there was very difficult. She felt like the walls, the floor, the ceiling, all were closing in on her. She would be trapped here forever, in a memory that was never authentic, that never held any meaning for the other person.

Rahul's betrayal was equally brutal for Amir. Even though he got justice, he never got closure. The once happy guy who was always ready to meet new people now shuts people out. This shift in his personality also caused him to suffer at his job.

Making connections and networking was essential to his job as an estate agent. Since he hadn't been able to sell a house for months, he was on the verge of being fired.

Everything seemed to be going in a decline. Sara and Amir were both drained of their energy. It is important to note that Sara and Amir were quite opposite.

Sara liked being on her own. She was an introvert, and when she opened up to Greg, she had to put herself out there. This betrayal had destroyed her peace of mind.

Amir was different. He was always willing to connect with others around him. He adored being around people and making friends at the drop of a hat. Trusting came easy to him, so when he signed the check for Rahul, fraud, scam, or theft never entered his mind.

Despite being so different when they faced betrayal, they shared similar feelings.

Shock and Denial.

It was hard for them both to see any light beyond this darkness that engulfed them.

Sara and Amir went through the shared pain of betrayal and hurt in their shattered world. The two broken souls stood on the rooftops of their buildings, looking at the moon they shared, although miles apart from each other.

The hustle and bustle of the city looked surreal to them. It was as if the world had decided to move on, leaving them both behind. The town was lit up with nightlights everywhere. As people below enjoyed the beginning of their weekend, Sara and Amir wondered if they could ever find a way out of this darkness.

The two had hit rock bottom.

# Chapter 3: Seeking Redemption

Getting back up from rock bottom isn't easy.

But that doesn't mean it is impossible.

They say, "When there is a will, there is a way," which is the absolute truth!

Dealing with adversities in life means there will be times when you will experience breakdowns. Some people have multiple breakdowns while fighting the challenges of their lives; for others, one is enough to jolt them awake and bring them back on track.

Remember, it doesn't matter how long it rains; a few drops of water are enough to sprout the seed of hope.

Still, how do you get there? Where is the road map? Are there any blueprints?

Let's take it step by step.

First and foremost, you need to decide you want to heal. There is nothing others can do to make you take this first step.

It is all on you.

You may find inspiration from others, but it is within yourself that you will find the power to overcome your life's biggest challenge. You see, it is only you who knows your struggle. Others may be able to sympathize, but seldom do you find people who can truly step into your shoes and empathize with you.

Moreover, if there is anyone you should trust to help you come out of this catastrophe, it is yourself.

The first person to rely on is you. Hence, you must stand tall and offer a hand to yourself.

This conscious choice to heal is critical because it helps gain the confidence that one has lost. Moreover, that willpower is what you need to get back up on your feet.

Sara knew she had no one but herself. Her parents lived far away, and she hadn't been out with her friends for a long time. Even though Sara's best friend would message her, trying to coax her out of the new apartment, Sara wouldn't respond.

It was the same for Amir. He could not get closure despite having a solid circle of supporters, friends, and family. People had lied to him before, but Rahul's betrayal had touched a nerve for some reason. It immensely affected him. It was about not being able to judge a person accurately.

Nothing others said would help them heal. Until one morning, Sara woke up to see a rainbow in the sky. The previous night had been gloomy and dark. It had rained the entire time, and heavy, grey clouds seemed to take over the city.

Sara thought the sun wouldn't shine again, but the following day, the sight of the bright sun and a mesmerizing rainbow made her realize something.

Light will always overpower darkness. A new dawn WILL rise, no matter how long the night seems.

Seeing the beautiful sunny day made Sara genuinely smile after days. She breathed in the fresh air and decided to go for a run. For some odd reason, this ordinary day felt like it was special. Just a slight change in perception helped Sara find hope inside her.

It can be hard to find hope in the dark. It will feel like your soul is staggering around, looking for something to hold on to. Then, finally, you see that light. You move forward and grasp it. It glows around you. If you keep holding on to it, hope lights up the darkness that fills you.

Sara grabbed onto the hope she had found in her. She quickly grabbed her shoes and began running without thinking about where she was headed. She took this precious time to lock away all the negative thoughts she had in her mind. She took in the world around her. People walking around, off to work or to run errands; children holding their parent's hands -some meekly looking at her, passing a sweet smile, some up to mischief while their parents ran after them.

The shops welcomed customers, and people shopped around. Some young college students were hanging around a coffee place, wearing their Ivy League jackets, scrolling on their phones.

A community of people, bustling here and there. The noise and momentum caused her to feel that there was so much more to this life. As she ran ahead, she came across a small, old bookshop. She felt drawn to it. This little bookshop looked familiar among all these shiny, new, crowded shops: isolated in a corner, ignored, and living in its little bubble, just like Sara. She could see herself in the glass window and suddenly stopped.

This shop was unique and special. It had a rustic charm that other places didn't have. It was novel and added allure to the street. Sara had forgotten this about herself. Just because she didn't like going around or preferred to be alone didn't mean she wasnt special. She had been comparing herself with other girls that Greg was cheating on her with. Sara thought she was the problem. But that wasn't true.

Sara walked in and was instantly taken by the warm atmosphere. It felt like she had walked in through a portal.

All those people who couldn't see the bookshop didn't have the eye. Sara wondered why the owner didn't close the shop as new bright stores started popping up around it. They didn't change what was special about them so that they could keep up. The owner understood that the loyal customers valued this tiny shop with a cozy ambiance and the familiar smell of books.

"Ah, a new face today! How may I help you, young lady?" asked an elderly man from behind the counter.

The happy and expectant face of this man made Sara smile. "I need something to write in. A nice thick notebook," she replied.

"A lot on your mind?" he asked, making conversation.

"I suppose, yeah," she answered. She had been thinking about her a lot as she ran. As she observed life around her, she knew she needed to change things. She was ready to begin a new chapter in her life. She was determined and wanted to make the most of this energy.

As the man guided her toward the notebooks, her eyes landed on a few self-help books. She picked out a few that looked interesting and chose the notebook with the most pages. She was ready to begin a new journey.

Coincidentally, on the same street, He had been showing a lavish apartment in a skyscraper to a couple. He had been pushing himself lately because he had no energy to interact with people. He didn't want to make the effort to make connections anymore because he thought they were useless.

As the couple looked around the apartment, Amir observed the life below from the humongous windows.

The streets were alive with the pulse of the city. Like specks of life, people moved with purpose, and buildings stretched into the sky, reaching for unseen heights. Yet, amidst this vibrant panorama, Amir felt disconnected, a mere observer of a world he no longer felt a part of.

The encounter with betrayal had left him questioning the authenticity of connections. His once exuberant spirit had been replaced by a weariness that settled deep within. The couple before him marveled at the luxurious apartment, discussing its features and envisioning a future within those walls. Amir, however, was caught in a moment of introspection, an inadvertent pause in the rhythm of his life.

The same rainbow that helped Sara take her first step was staring at Amir and welcoming him toward enlightenment. The only problem was that Amir felt so disconnected from the world that even the glorious sight of the mesmerizing sky couldn't pull him back up to his feet.

People don't miraculously change their perceptions in seconds. For Sara, her thoughts and observations led her to believe that she needed to heal. Unfortunately, it wasnt the case with Amir.

Amir's friends had been trying to get in touch with him. They wanted to help him and offer support. When Amir was surviving with the bit of money he had left, his true friends offered to help him financially. His boss, who was fond of Amir, understood that he needed some time off.

This meeting was the first time he interacted with clients after the court hearings and winning the case. He tried socializing with the couple similarly but couldn't muster the same enthusiasm.

It is essential to understand that Amir wasn't depressed. He wasn't sad about losing the money.

He was hurt. He was shaken by the fact that the connections he had made over the years were meaningless. This episode had left him feeling dumb.

His mind was a whirlwind of conflicting emotions. He replayed the moments of betrayal, questioning the authenticity of every smile, every shared laugh. The rainbow, once a symbol of hope, now felt like a cruel trick played by the universe. His struggle was internal, and the city below, vibrant and alive, seemed oblivious to his pain.

The couple liked the apartment but felt it was out of budget. The old Amir could have easily convinced them. It would have thrilled him to show them more apartments and help them decide the best place to call home.

But he nodded, "We will get in touch again when we find something."

He left the building and walked toward his car. Suddenly, he bumped into a woman walking out of a bookshop. The shopping bag in her hands fell out of her hands, and books were everywhere on the ground.

"I am so sorry. I wasn't really looking where I was going," Amir apologized as he bent down to pick up the books.

"I know that feeling," said the woman quietly with a short smile. Her eyes and smile looked familiar to Amir. They were eyes that hid their pain. As Amir gathered the books, a quote on a book cover caught his eye.

> *"Take the first step in faith. You don't have to see the whole staircase, just take the first step."*
>
> - Martin Luther King Jr.

"That's the one that caught my eye too," she said shyly.

He reread the last part. Just take the first step.

He didn't know what to say. He looked at the young girl and felt something in his stomach. It wasn't anything complex like love at first sight.

It was simply the feeling of making a new connection.

"Yeah, I think…I needed that," he replied, conscious that his mouth was splitting into a smile.

"You should buy one for yourself then," she encouraged Amir.

"I actually think, I will," he answered, handing her the books.

"Anyway, thanks!" she said, holding the books with a stronghold. She began walking away.

"I…I didn't catch your name?" he called.

"Sara," she stated nervously, looking back and walking away.

Amir suddenly felt light. It had only been a few seconds of interaction, but the rawness of this encounter had opened something in his heart.

He looked at the shop Sara had walked out of and was surprised to see the old bookshop on a fancy street. He had never even noticed it was there.

He decided to buy the book he had just seen, the one with the quote. He walked into the shop and was greeted by an older man who guided him toward the self-help books.

Amir grabbed a few titles, including the one he had seen Sara buy. Smiling, he left the shop. It seemed Amir had found a purpose in life. He understood that he needed to work on some things and was inviting change to kickstart this journey.

As Amir devoured the books, so did Sara in the other corner of town.

Amir and Sara had no connections and lived far apart, but the universe has ways of playing tricks on us. Sometimes, these tricks help us, and other times, they lead us to many troubles, but somehow, some way, it's all a part of finding ourselves.

The universe planned Sara and Amir's chance encounter; however brief it may be, it helped them both start their journey of redemption.

You see, it was out of the ordinary for Sara to converse with a random stranger. Similarly, it wasn't like Amir to believe in self-help books. Still, something at that moment had convinced him to. They both were beginning a journey to heal and rejuvenate.

# Chapter 4: The Power of Resilience

Sara was excited to begin her journey to heal. In one of the books, she had read that to let go of her negative emotions, she needed to write them down.

So, she was curled up on her couch with a blanket, scribbling away in her new journal.

Negative thoughts are a part of the human condition. Even the most positive minds are sometimes engulfed with negative emotions and vibes. This can build up rage inside of us.

Some people are more patient and can tame this rage for quite some time. But just like blowing air into a balloon, there is a limit to all this rage building up. Sure enough, they soon pop like a balloon, and all that patience disappears in anguish.

Instead, investing your energy in a more fruitful activity is best. Now, this doesn't mean being patient is bad. Patience is a virtue many struggle to adopt, but those who are blessed with it should use it wisely.

Use your patience in your healing process.

The journal felt like an empty vessel she was ready to fill, a friend she was prepared to rant with. Her friends couldn't understand why Sara took so long to get over this breakup.

Wasn't it just a regular part of everyone's life?

Seldom do you find your soul mate in one try, they would say.

What they didn't understand was that people go through grief in different ways. For them, a breakup might not be a big deal. However, baring her soul and seeing a partner in someone wasn't easy for Sara.

Sara took a sip from her coffee cup. The living room was filled with the robust aroma of the hot beverage. The dusky light of the sunset was seeping in through the blinds. Sara placed her coffee cup on the table and returned to writing.

Was I not enough? she wrote.

This nagging thought had been on her mind. People often engage in self-criticism when they go through a tragedy. For some reason, finding fault in themselves is easier than looking at the situation from a different perspective. Of course, there are plenty of other factors at play here, but it is pretty standard to blame themselves

The second negative statement she wrote was:

Will I ever be able to find my true love?

What is life without a companion? Many people believe it is not just a romantic partner humans crave. People need connections, platonic ones, too, to keep them going. Humans thrive with connections; it gives them a sense of belonging. And so, this statement by Sara isn't surprising; it is simply a human need that she needs to fulfill.

One crucial aspect of penning down your negative thoughts is not judging yourself. As mentioned earlier, negative thoughts are a part of us, and there should be no shame in expressing them in a healthy way.

The journal was an outlet for Sara to express her feelings and validate her emotions. It was a cathartic experience that was going to help reduce her stress and anxiety as she moved forward in her journey.

Journaling is considered one of the best ways to begin your journey of self-discovery. Healing lies in answers you search for in yourself. The questions only you can answer. Self-help books, much like this one, can guide you to begin this process and maintain discipline in following through. However, you must hold yourself accountable and confront your truths.

Just like Sara, you, too, can begin your healing process and enter this new world of journaling.

When researching journaling, you might see some highly elaborate examples. People use their journals to express all sorts of feelings. People don't just rant; they draw, illustrate, sketch, paint, doodle, write poetry, and reflect in various ways.

You might discover some super pristine, aesthetically pleasing, and artistic journals. But do not be overwhelmed by this. Journals can be a mess, too. After all, that is how your mind, body, and soul are initially. Don't be too hard on yourself if your journal doesn't look like a professional artist has been sketching in it.

Your journal is focused on you; thus, it is different for everyone. Sara has added many sticky notes in her journal with positive affirmations written on them. She uses them to remind herself that she is worthy of all good things in life. It boosts her self-worth and helps her be less judgemental towards herself.

If you want to start journaling, start with writing your heart out. Every night, before you sleep, put on a timer of 5 minutes and simply write. Give the overthinking a rest by pouring it all out on paper.

Remember, you don't necessarily have to write with your hand. Although writing can be a therapeutic experience, you can always open a blank document on your laptop and start writing.

Initially, you might stare at the screen or paper, wondering what to write. Don't worry, and start by describing your surroundings.

Where are you sitting?

Describe the setting of the room.

What's the weather like?

What do you expect will happen when you finish writing?

This is just freestyle writing. You are not looking for a breakthrough. You are simply getting rid of the burden of the day or celebrating your triumphs.

As you move forward in your journaling journey, lose the judgment. Tell the critique in your mind to take a seat, then lock the door and throw away the keys.

When you write, try not to censor yourself. No feeling is bad; no thoughts are evil. Let it all out on paper (or screen), and let it flow out of your mind.

If freestyle writing isn't your thing, you can use prompts to help you kickstart the process.

Here are a few journaling prompts that Sara looked up to help her through her breakup:

1. What do you not miss about your ex?
2. What were the red flags you didn't recognize?
3. What's something you always wanted to do but couldn't because of your ex?
4. Why do you deserve a new start?
5. How would you like to spend your day?
6. What are three things you are grateful for?
7. How are you feeling right now?

These are just a few examples. You can alter them as per your preferences, or you can look up more prompts that can be helpful in your situation.

A thought-provoking prompt is to step into the other person's shoes. This helps build empathy and set a path for forgiveness. However, this comes later in the process. In the beginning, it is best to focus on yourself.

When writing out your innermost emotions, it is best to avoid rereading your entries. The point of writing out all these negative thoughts and feelings is to let them go. So don't revisit those emotions this way.

Sara has been regularly writing in the journal for the past week. She finds it to be a great way to let it all go. However, today, as she returned from her new place of work to an empty house, she suddenly felt empty again.

She didn't know what to do. She had been feeling great for the last few days, and journaling had played a significant role in helping her reach this point. She thought she was recovering, but here she was again.

Gloomy and dreadful.

Now, it might seem like Sara was going backward, but the truth is that healing and self-discovery take time. It is a long process, and at times, you might wonder how you are still battling the same demons, but fear not; you are on your way to a new self, a new you.

As they say, *"Trust the process."*

Now, the journal was right there in her usual place. Sara had deliberately placed it in the living room, where she spent most of her time. The journal was on the window bench, with a pen tucked in so she could grab it instantly whenever needed.

So, as usual, she fixed herself a cup of hot coffee and took to her journal. She could have gone through her previous entries. All it required was a flip.

But she didn't do it.

Instead, she turned to a blank page and used that to remember what she was grateful for. Moreover, she wrote about the new things she had learned about herself in this process. It had only been a few days, but she was already amazed at the amount of stress lifted off her shoulders.

Conflicts are a part of our life. What matters most is how we deal with the grief and sorrows of our lives.

While Sara found solace in the written word, Amir could not say the same. He struggled with expressing himself through the written words. He tried writing but found it difficult to say what he wanted.

It was a strange feeling for him, considering he once used his words to reach out to people in the most empathetic way. He was still the same on the inside. He had just lost that person somewhere.

Trust is a delicate thing. Those who are generous with it have more chances of hurting themselves. While making connections and forming relationships is important, it is essential to evaluate the people we are putting our trust in.

Are they even worthy of your trust?

Now, here is the thing. Intentions matter a lot. If your intentions are good, you hold no responsibility for how the other person acted.

How is Amir at fault for what Rahul did?

Amir is accountable for his actions, but trusting or putting your faith in someone is not bad. Most times, we cannot recognize the red flags in other people. We cannot see how some friends are only there when they need us and not vice versa. At times, we choose to unsee these things, and other times, we are too blinded by the fact that others may have bad intentions for us.

Well, if nothing, it is a sign of a pure heart.

Expecting good in people is human nature and makes us who we are—intelligible creatures who depend on empathy for survival.

Amir was in a debacle. He wasn't sure how to proceed. The self-help books talked about meditation, but Amir was spectacle about it.

Could it work? he wondered. He didn't think this was a very good idea for someone whose brain was constantly buzzing with thoughts.

Then, Amir remembered the young girl he had met. For some odd reason, she had become a beacon of hope for him. He had met her by chance and was grateful to the universe for sending a guardian angel. This wasn't some crush that Amir had formed. He had connected with a human being going through the same struggles.

He had noticed the pain in her eyes and could associate with someone on a deeper level after a long time. Amir may have incredible networking skills, but he only had a handful of people he connected with emotionally. This chance encounter had seemed spiritual for him. He felt the universe calling out to him. The vibes he had felt with her were astronomically peculiar.

He decided to give meditation a chance, just like the universe was giving him a chance to heal, a little hope to hold on to.

It was early morning, and the day had only just begun. The sunlight poured into the grand balcony of Amir's apartment. He didn't have a yoga mat or any outdoor furniture. The chilly wind embraced Amir as he sat on the floor. He looked at the towering skyscrapers around the building and wondered about every single life in them. Hundreds of stories were being played out, all different people fighting through their lives in their own ways.

He put a 5-minute timer on his phone and placed it beside him. Amir closed his eyes and took in all the noise, although there barely was any. He could hear the dogs barking and the dog walker calling, "Good dogs! You are all such good dogs."

He could also smell the fresh bread his neighbor baked every other day. She often shared some with him. He thought about making some garlic butter to go with it. He could hear the dad next door waking up his kids for school.

We are making multiple connections, even when we don't know it. Connecting with the universe isn't difficult. All you need to do is be mindful.

Listen to the sounds around you, feel the vibrations of the ground. There are so many ways you can relate to the people around you. Amir chose to use his senses during meditation. It was his first time, so blocking the noise wasn't required. Instead, he decided to embrace it and engage with it.

The alarm rang out, interrupting Amir's thoughts.

He opened his eyes. Everything looked the same. Nothing had changed, but for some odd reason. It had given Amir a little bit of peace.

He inhaled deeply, and something shifted in him as he exhaled. He suddenly felt lonely. For someone who constantly had people around him, isolation was highly uncomfortable.

For months now, he had been on his own, and the loneliness hit him right in his heart. It felt like his body had been lacking this connection. When he noticed the presence around him, his body suddenly realized what had been missing.

Perhaps his soul had been in shock, and the emptiness Amir felt brought him here.

Amir sat there, the lingering feeling of loneliness casting a shadow over the peace he had momentarily found.

It was a paradoxical moment; he had stumbled upon an unsettling truth in seeking solace through meditation. The void within him, previously masked by constant activity and social engagements, was now quite apparent.

For months now, Amir had embraced this isolation, but now it felt like an unveiled guest causing a looming shadow over him.

The realization hit him like a wave, and for a moment, he grappled with the discomfort of solitude.

As Amir sat on his balcony, surrounded by the sounds of the waking city, he pondered the significance of this newfound awareness.

What was he going to do with this awareness?

He wanted to give these feelings some time to settle in. So, Amir decided to begin every day by meditating the same way. He also decided to research more regarding meditation.

The following day, he closed his eyes again, not to shut out the world but to confront the emptiness within. He acknowledged the loneliness in the stillness, allowing it to wash over him like a gentle tide. It was a challenging acknowledgment, for Amir was a man who thrived on connections, on the bustling energy of human interactions.

The second meditation session proved to be a journey into self-discovery in a different light. Amir wasn't seeking an escape; instead, he was confronting the solitude.

The practice of mindfulness, which had initially seemed like an escape, soon became a mirror reflecting the void he had been avoiding.

It had been a whole week of meditating, and as the timer signaled the end of the session on a Sunday morning, Amir opened his eyes with a newfound understanding. He realized that meditation was not about escaping the world but diving deep within it. It was a tool for self-exploration.

Amir's skepticism toward meditation had transformed into a willingness to explore this inner journey further.

Like Amir, many people think meditation is bogus, but alas, they don't understand the beauty of it.

It's a profound exploration into the depths of one's existence, a journey that requires patience, openness, and a willingness to embrace both the light and the shadows within.

Amir had been researching more about meditation and was highly intrigued by mindfulness.

Mindfulness is different from what Amir had been doing. There are other forms of meditation, and it is good to explore different ways of meditation. This will help you find what is right for you.

Here are a few different forms of meditation:

- Mindfulness meditation
- Yoga
- Focused meditation
- Guided meditation
- Movement meditation

Amir was inclined toward mindfulness, which requires you to focus on your breathing and guide your mind back when it wanders. Overthinking or a continuous chain of thoughts is quite common, which you will experience the first time you meditate. The act of bringing your focus back to breathing improves focus.

Emptying your mind or avoiding distracting thoughts is quite a challenge for beginners, but don't worry; you will get there eventually.

The most important thing is to remember not to judge yourself during this process. The aim is simple: To acknowledge the present and anchor yourself in the moment.

Furthermore, it also focuses on bringing yourself back into the moment.

With that said, you shouldn't expect meditation to make your problems disappear magically. It can, however, help you get the space you need. Regularly meditating can bring long-lasting beneficial changes in your life.

Let's take you through the step-by-step process of mindfulness meditation:

1.  Locate a spot that resonates with calmness and tranquility. If you are a beginner, start with a brief duration, five or 10 minutes.
2.  Sit comfortably—whether in a chair, loosely cross-legged, or kneeling—ensuring stability for an extended session.
3.  Connect with the sensation of your breath, embracing each inhalation and exhalation.
4.  As your mind inevitably drifts away, perhaps in seconds, minutes, or five minutes, gently guide your focus back to the breath.
5.  Avoid self-judgment or fixating on the content of your fleeting thoughts. Simply return.
6.  When you feel ready, lift your gaze or open your eyes if closed. Take a moment to attune to the surrounding sounds, assess your current bodily sensations, and acknowledge your thoughts and emotions.

It is this simple. Direct your attention, allow your mind to wander, bring it back, and approach the process with utmost kindness, repeating as needed.

Now, the question most people ask is how much I should meditate. The answer is very straightforward. As much as you like, as many times as you like.

Amir likes to meditate every morning without fail, and experts do recommend the same, even if it is for five minutes.

However, if you struggle with consistency, don't fret. Create your plan. Some people like doing it in bed, right before they sleep. It helps them let go of the stress of the day.

When you decide to sit and meditate, you have already crossed the first step. Encourage yourself and ensure you are giving yourself a judgment-free space. You would be surprised at how critical we can be of ourselves even when we don't mean to be.

At this point, Sara and Amir have both learned to love their scars. They understand that these scars are a part of them but do not define who they are. That's for them to decide.

Now, how do they piece themselves together? How do they put together that broken soul?

That is the real question, is it not?!

# Chapter 5: Piecing it Together

[content to be created]

# Chapter 6: Rising Above

[content to be created]

# Chapter 7: From Brokenness to Empowerment

[content to be created]